AF255868

GNASHING TEETH
PUBLISHING
words that get in your teeth

TELEPATH

Inception 1

  The Bill Collectors 3

  Guessing Weight 4

  Mentalist Act 5

  First Contact 7

  The Invaders 8

  Babel 9

  Swedish 10

  Alien Abduction 11

  UAP 12

  HEAR 13

  Hope and Gwendolyn 14

  Sending and Receiving 15

  Night Scares 17

  Taxi 18

  The Pigeon Ladies 19

  Star of Hope 21

  My mother, she ate me 22

  SEEK 23

  Paratransit 24

  Tatya 25

  Knowing versus Being 26

  Yoruba 27

  telepath enslaved 28

  her drunk father 29

  Bid Whist 30

  WBSU 32

  Feats of Prowess 34

  different skills 35

  MIND 36

  Telepathist 37

  The Cheaters 38

Irish 39

Failed Spy 40

Rabbit 41

Romeo and Juliet 42

Cat Dreams 43

MIND 44

Debridement 45

WHOGOESTHERE 46

Telepath's Guy 47

Priestess 48

SEEK 50

How This Is 51

I 53

II 54

III 55

IV 56

V 57

VI 58

VII 59

Transit Called Dreaminess 61

A Mercury Sextile Neptune 63

The Singer 64

Portal 66

Ignite 67

Encompass 68

T- Stroll 69

Acknowledgments 71

Telepath Notes 72

About the Author 76

Inception

The Bill Collectors

We always knew before the phone rang
who was calling if we knew the person
and we knew when we didn't know
and didn't want to answer:
probably a bill collector and so a hasty
script devised: No, this was not the head of the house.
No, our parents were indisposed —
a word we relished because it meant on the toilet
Or they had just left for the bank or store
or some errand we children were not privy to
And yes, we were armed, and unafraid
of their insinuations of neglect.
Don't try to outsmart us,
you are not our first white bill collector
and we have a history of dodging bullets
if not chains.

Guessing Weight

The Carny can't guess my weight.
He is a native used to looking at white people.
He does not know my dark density.
No number can express what I am packed with.
Besides, there is my face,
looking 20 years younger
than the calendar predicts, telling him
that he won't, and can't ever know.
He grins, defiant, already seduced, and wrong –
these generations and generations of self upon self.
These are heavy bones, even if I move lightly,
dodge tackles down the field, split to the floor,
bike, sprint, swim: generations of water crossers
island folk, weight bearers, spin within.
He looks in my eyes
and is hypnotized by my transparency.
He fails,   and I win a big, fluffy bear
that I give to a niece.

Mentalist Act

Their act was different, daring
She was caramel, a stunner, whose
gift arrived as pubescent protection
from preying pedophiles planning to pounce
on her early-arriving prodigious pulchritude

She could hear and reflexively listened
never walking some concrete alone,
knowing day could hold more danger than night
in a mega city whose rhythms emptied
some thoroughfares during office hours,
less trafficked than when denizens of the dark patrolled

She watched Nightmare Alley and crafted her act
with a friend, a beard, a foil, a wingman
They needed no code, no watch for her to finger
the blindfold was an aid, a comfort, cutting out
distracting stimuli of audience gasps or leers
ever ready to razz or jeer from thin, drooling lips

The collected cufflink, bracelet, gold chain
were only compass needles guiding her
straight to lying brains, lusts and denials

She had to learn discretion, to not blurt out
the glimpsed horrors, they paid to be revealed
but only so much to avoid reprisals
an ankle for the long skirted
a calf curve for the short, the barest bit of
a psyche's cleavage, a clavicle, a caress

Slashing through each night's muck
and mania paid her bills
occasionally, she could rake a bit of it,
pass a rogue insight on to an equalizer,
clean up a corner of the world

vestigial skills
telepathic atrophy
we're lonely apart

First Contact

Telepaths were sent there first
Aliens met our true inner selves
Minds were undone in starburst

Our best attributes and our worst
made transparent to those who delved
telepaths, sadly, were sent there first

Practiced scripts, undone, now unrehearsed
we revealed deeply flawed and wretched selves
our minds were undone in starburst

We wonder now if we've been cursed
hierarchy stored high upon back shelves
Telepaths, sadly, were sent there first

Wounded pride has since been nursed
hubris deep within us dwells
our minds unfurled in starburst

Knowledge, for which we hunger and thirst
denied after they read inside our cells
Telepaths were sent there first
minds were unmasked in starburst

The Invaders

Telepaths do not self-identify
wise enough to know the danger
already predicted by movie makers.
Any can guess how they'd be used—

Still, how to warn the world of danger,
walking among its masses
growing in number and strength,
visible though, in ways too subtle

How they don't register, their static,
not the song of human thoughts that hum
or sing or clang, but always share short clarity,
but not their blur-beclouded minds

that move in another dimension's time,
though encased, embodied by fleshy shells
here, their alien vegetable thoughts
move through an elsewhere,
and only telepaths can discern their crimes

Babel

Our original language was electric thought
our egos led us toward that realm on high
It was not Eden alone where sin was brought
and the Lord divided us, as we mounted the sky.

Our egos led us toward that realm on high.
Our collective will broken, we were struck down
and the Lord divided us as we mounted the sky
one nation of all crumbled to many towns.

Our collective will broken, we were struck down
scattered across the world, dissolved our precious unity
one nation of all crumbled to many towns.
Remnants of our oneness now called telepathy.

Scattered across the world, dissolved unity
bred the rise of strife and vile royal hierarchies.
Remnants of our oneness now called telepathy.
Our collective conscious shred by the Lord's enmity.

Bred the rise of strife and vile royal hierarchies
feudal dominions and violent tribal conflicts.
Our collective conscious shred by the Lord's enmity
our lost oneness smashed to frayed, failed bits.

Feudal dominions and violent tribal conflicts
slowed our ascent up the astral way.
We fought to maintain our frayed failed bits
telepathic conduits seen in Egyptian hieroglyphics.

Our slowed ascent up the astral way
traversing ley lines, warp and weft of earth's loom
telepathic conduits found in Egyptian hieroglyphics.
We work and weave to reconnect, avert possible doom.

Swedish

To be telepathic, "telepatisk", "läsa tankar" (eng:to read minds)
To be a telepath, "telepat", "tankeläsare" (eng:mindreader)

Alien Abduction

why are we taken
upgrade for telepathy
undo Babel's curse

UAP

only their rebels respond
the others keep their thoughts to themselves,
each other, never reaching out, or to,
knowing how much they must slow
and simplify, amused or bemused
how a glimpse of a vehicle
overhead, makes our thoughts
swarm like ants at a picnic
around a piece of cake

HEAR
ECHO
AHAS
ROSE

Hope and Gwendolyn

The way her mother and aunt had visits
always joyful greetings at the door
But no one remembered why she was there
or what words passed between them
if any… her Auntie entered, may have eaten cake
with coffee or her Pepsi, smoked, drawing elegantly
exhaling artfully, spoke with Mommy, no one knew
and didn't know that they didn't know, until the afterglow
when Daddy would say they communicated without sound
the children, the family were right there, in their orbit
on a parallel plane left out of those private conversations

Sending and Receiving
for Leslie Walker

Leslie and I tried to send symbols
to people we never met, whose names
we'd never know, whose faces we would not
learn to forget, at appointed times,
or wait in cleared readiness to receive
what was on the cards: stars
are all I remember, experimenting
reaching past the grass squares
bound by chain link fences between our small homes
rutted streets of access, we fled as soon
as we could, forward, projecting more,
receiving possibilities, imagining distant others

My partner in-flight willing
to imagine with me: I was never
deemed weird or cast out, only
taken in, abetted, aided, and we saw
the film of our lives rewind, an accident,
unhappen, the bike wheel spun with
our longing to move the world closer
to our hearts and needs, a response
to girl power marshaled in backyards.

She was up for flight and down for doing
venturing on two Q buses to Jamaica subway
to another world, parallel, great Gotham, immediately
faster, bigger, breathtaking
thinking through time, leaping distances

Through the Queens dark, from
the front-facing bedroom window
a slanted roof my cousin climbed out on
leapt down from, fled, that held the night sky
above the scent of trees and lingering dinners
and two short, A-framed stories, full of stars

Maybe that was the wrong direction
out, onward, but I faced it, sending
receiving, trying to transmit. Delicious
memory, out, out and   away

Night Scares

We were frightened awake
by encyclopedias and novels
leaping off shelves in the middle of the night

crashing loudly to the parquet floor
not from the ends but the middles
they flew by ones and by twos

Father said, fear not
It is your own young teen self, growing
up, reaching out, grabbing books, making a mess
as usual

Taxi

Later, they told her that her first word was taxi
a true New Yorker cradled in their startled arms
Not the first unnerving she delivered
staring at them as if they were aliens, they recalled,
which, of course, they were, to her, newly arrived
unaccustomed to this set up, two semi-mute,
bleating beings working so hard for their upkeep
making music and exchanging meaning with their bodies
kissing and holding her and taking her to others,
ah more yes, this was more like what she was forgetting,
elders, aunt, uncles, family, to translate her better,
but still not quite receiving her either
figuring out how to help this pair bond,
how to be with them,
this was what they wanted with a clear urgency
in the city's leaning cold and dark,
to go back to their small, warm place
where she made three in a blue heaven,
summon a way to get there:
Taxi! she yelled at 6 months,
forgetting herself
and seeing their fright,
shut up 'til a more acceptable age.

The Pigeon Ladies

I would wriggle to create a truce
between the bloom of crinoline netting
at the back of tender legs
and stray jabbing strands of frayed basketweave
on subway seat cushions
and settle by my mother's side
for we had places to go
people to see, mountains to climb
and worlds to conquer
Invariably a pigeon lady, as my brother and I
named them, would alight next to me
mounds of chest flesh feathered in floral dresses
with pale faces and strange accents.

They would tell me their life stories
pouring out unintelligible feelings
too alien for my child decipherment
though not understanding, I listened.
And at the end of their confessions,
their myths and tales recounted
they offered candy that I had been taught to refuse

But over my head, to my mother/father
one asked if she could offer, it was wrapped
making some pronouncement about me,
and perhaps my future, having visited
some interior part of me yet to be known,
or maybe a past familiar self,

perhaps, it was just that she,
an escapee from European wars and woes,
without her birth language, had, in this huge foreign city,
felt something deep and real for a little black girl
a kinship through the rumble and sigh of the train

My parents always politely refused
While I ever wondered how it came to be
in those fields of dress and coat pockets

and sometimes worn dark handbags with short strap handles,
that the pigeon women walked the city
provisioned with sweets.

Star of Hope

My mother asked me if I could
help her love—my father—and I shook
with this acknowledgment of possibility:
what was she telling me about my ability,
something imagined or real? I only knew
our connection by its flaking detritus.

Galaxies away, he knew when my life
was threatened, he knew when my heart
broke against the stone of institutional
denials, when my dream of medicine
was slain, when I almost slid off
a mountain in a rogue spring snowstorm.

He felt me writhe, shed and strain
against radioactive pain, my hard head
bruised, blistered, bled. But I was a child
who couldn't feel where he was hurt
nor fix it. Perhaps that blue barrier
was his love, perhaps that's what
all good parents do, charge us
up, fill our soul battery, direct
current ever forward, forging onward.

So I focused on him. She died, a
fissile incandescence, resonating
her stone-lifting, infrasonic fragrance
illuminating in her decohering departure
as her children procreate, learn, warp on.

My mother, she ate me

Our mother was always eating us
She ate me
She ate all her babies, she said proudly
through her we came and
to her we might return, in bits

She made us and would
tell me *I brought you*
into this world and I can
take you out of it

One of her many threats
wipe that smile off your face
watch your mouth
fix your face
which was hard to do having been bitten
but good therianthropic training
for my shapeshifting future

I had a father too
he could fix many things and my face
He was brave and would do this
while she was looking
but not so she could see

would tell me in my head
it's okay baby, I got you
holding a buffer pattern
of my original whole
so I could be reconstituted
and transmitted forward

SEEK
ELSE
ESSE
KEEP

Paratransit

This taxi driver saved skunk babies
nurtured them till they could forage
feed themselves, on crops and garbage

Saved for wife and a little home
that should've been theirs after renting to own
hard lessons learned of money and trust
how to earn and not get burned

He saw that hole in a Big Flats hill
that was not always there
saw high ruins of a moon mill
that for our eyes alone, appeared

told me about rattlers in land's rise,
and then those secrets in our sky
floating city ships that sang above
the concrete ribbon that we rode

and in fluffed mounds of clouds, appeared
a shapely something in bright air
tethered to our everywhere
layers only we perceived and shared

Tatya

Tatya the telepath tried to figure out which game show to go on. she considered carefully the vulnerability of hosts, their readability; did the cards hold the answer? On Jeopardy, how empty might their minds be? For a Funny You Should Ask; how easy it was to discern the liars as she watched, not using any particular ability. She'd have to visit that show to be certain. Contestant against contestant, could she pluck right answers from their brains? Pictionary was fun, she could draw just a line and her team would answer indecipherable squiggles lasered straight to the sender's brain. Two loops for things in the living room lead to ceiling fan, a carton of milk, Milky Way, a funnel with circle for a telescope, 25 Words Or Less always had her betting two clues or less because there was nothing to guess. She dyed her hair red, cut it, wore a blue wig and then a grassy green one, adjusted her height with platforms or flats, changed her look with glasses and racked up the winnings.

mutable self plays
many games offer riches
uneasy gambles

Knowing versus Being

He's long dead now, way too soon,
so is the Alien Planetscapes friend that introduced you two
it was magical his boundless love of many musics
those great combinations he spun on those turntables in Jersey

How shocked his white buddy was at the sight of you
proving a point you could only guess, there were others
as you hung out, charmed, perfumed and kibbitzed

as night, dawn sounds shaped sea damp city air
from across the Hudson entering apartments' many ears
so when you say it is through, he flies over, enraged
the locked downstairs door is tricked, breached

'til he stands banging on your apartment door with his fists of fury
You see it shake, and move, refuse to face him,
wonder if you should call the cops
and know you couldn't know the outcome

for an angry young black man, no matter
that he drove subway trains, was good to his mother
respected his father, lived in their brownstone, maintained
a high standard of living, good city job and all

and DJ'd articulately, creating a graduate education in citizenship
and imagination's sweep and possibilities from Miles
to XTC to black forest folk chants to avant disco throat singing

Reading the anger is not controlling it
nor is knowing the unearned hate
and your consolation is that you did nothing
to hasten his untimely end

Yoruba

A Yorùbá elder was consulted and she said Arínúródé—which literally translates to "one who sees/reads the inside and reads the outside."

telepath enslaved

She couldn't decipher the enslaver's thoughts
His foreign words of abuse and fury
guessed only because she could smell the reek of harm,
nothing but a sulfurous, cold, hard rage.

Though she missed that any of the dark shadow
was directed at her, as the image he held within
rendered her unrecognizable to herself

She saw nothing in his mind's eye that resembled
her being was a thing, a blur
a receptacle that he would take, wrench

spend his pale coinage in the purloined purse
of her. She could untangle these thought forms
knotted, wriggling, warped before she understood them.

Her descendants knew the words and still tremble
at the veiled horror and savagery they hide
as terrible truths emanate and wound repeatedly.

They know when to avoid the empty bathroom,
of the suited, set around a corporate table,
nurses and doctors, waitstaff, and clerks,

colleagues dashing past in supermarket aisles,
eyes averted, thoughts Loud, the ambulance crew,
screaming at their injured need, only the gentle firemen
think help not harm. All these others leak
their clues. Her inheritors know how to avoid

the drugged drinks, those construction sites
with plywood barriers, the quiet country lane
empty of witness, the abandoning study group
leaving her bemused, battered, inheritor alone

her drunk father

You were a foil for your roommate
who used the apartment as a closet
and yet demanded things when she appeared
your fabric shears to cut her wayward hair

that you never tell her parents that she was rarely there
her boyfriend on west 106th just two blocks away
across 1970s Manhattan's Broadway

so it was not predictive skills that saved you
when her drunk father arrived and demanded
to wait for her return as you made excuses: grad school study
and you in the midst of a film collective meeting

You knew to beg your film group to stay,
and as fast hours slipped away,
one by one they left, until only Hassan remained
reading what you read: expel rogue father
else by dawn you would be dead or worse

Her drunk father could not be coerced,
but was persuaded to leave
before the last Long Island Railroad train
left for their benighted part of country Queens

and so you lived, unmarred by this
grateful to be heard, and saved

Bid Whist
for Marilyn Jean

She was a whiz at Bid Whist
She could count even while high
make these books of prowess
lateral towers of ownership
in the battle of wills and minds

Tournaments held in the BSU basement
at square card tables of four in
ivy league juke joints as onlookers
there gasped or sighed, ate, watched
minor magic, create and play

acquiring kings, queens, jacks, knights,
numbers, aces, spades, diamonds, jokers,
clubs, hearts, go uptown, downtown,
win to be the last team, all the why

I couldn't read even hearing
or understand even glimpsing
seeing can be believing,
but it's still not knowing how
to replicate, those most stunning moves

Her bright bravado earned by slick skill
practice made powerful protection
as strategy instructed dumb luck to witch wisdom

She did not influence the dealing, but could
the way her long, tapered, violinist fingers
made the cards flicker, slicing light and time
and sing, scatting the jazz of gamble

Restirring the possibilities
talk shit and smack like the guys
kick them right where their egos lied

Cards, read like bones or fortunes,
as she chose symbiotic partners
who fit her style, who led and followed,
darting as she did through bullshit shields
and wily rogue's defenses,

to arrive at her station as she bid it
as only a city girl could
command the vehicle of conveyance
to the next adventure, to arrive

A sight to behold this bold beauty,
in her cropped vest, shaped 'fro,
leonine face with those cat eyes
above squared cheekbones from her political mother
behind those large, trendsetting glasses

and that dazzling feline smile of menace and delight
as she consumed the energy of the moment and sparkled
with its transmutation, blazing in our conspiratorial dim
constructions of culture and connection
despite the oppositional cold: Bam! slap, snatch,
another book made, a winning hand

whose deep voice, crackled with her guttural chuckle,
        you fool you she would say affectionately
to my admiration

the thoughts she read, the known fake allowed to play
to set them up, a better track to pull that train

WBSU

Dissolve words   feel another language
your stilled tongue tastes light
your fractal momentum tunes to another frequency
let me take you higher   in the lit dim moment
as we foment underground
we are close to earth and calling up our energies

I want to take you higher
boom shaka laka laka boom shaka laka vortex dancing down
our higher selves soul group sweating
as we shook flesh to shape shift

higher higher higher,
ascending signal punctuating trumpet call
and angelic horns endowed with sacred fire
all elements at our gathering

higher higher all on the floor
all gathered all one
making water fall and burst into 1 million droplets

all one in our meaning/less/ness
boom shaka laka shaking off all definition
as we spun into fractals in that basement
consecrated with shared moment,
shared memory, electric momentum, conduits

all our bodies resonant with what waits beyond joy
before constraints, shimmering past denial,
we knew the place yeah, we took us there
ain't nobody worried ain't nobody crying

we took us there higher, higher,

as some leapt leapt leapt out of time into eternal continuity
all the darkness lit with our yearning endlessness

as the dance floor floated, crowded with ancestral reverberations
                    all our future pasts

revelations as we expended and fueled
creating our new our possibilities of meant to be
meant now our everbeings
our consecrated dreams   our joy in each other

sweat affirmations of oneness
                and spirit orbs   paused over mission park
                and lit the way back to our dorms
                                    higher

Feats of Prowess
for Dana

People deny what they see
that basketball all air
from an improbable distance
beyond half court, into the netted hoop,
& that unstoppable run, zigzagging,
down field, untackled, erect, triumph
and workers labored, laundered, ate
near improbable megaton pyramids, proof,
a choir of psyches was needed to augment
and orchestrate muscles, yes, yes, bodies
are used, trained, housing minds that learn
dazzling me with their prowess, stunning
uncomprehending you

different skills

Who does the medium read
when reporting from the dead
is it something wreathed about you
dwelling in your heart or your head

are they reading traceries you emanate
or is it always some red shifted other
engraved gone energies
of father, sister, brother, mother

are they your own soul messages you send
or is it really not the now
but of an ever without end?

MIND
IDEA
NEAR
DARE

Telepathist

When others' emanations reveal their secret truths
which unbidden, arrive as rogue, unannounced guests
disrobe their social lies, their grim, hidden views
when others' emanations reveal their secret truths
their oblique assessments and distortions of you
which disrupt, yet arm you to pass condescending tests
when others' emanations revealed their nasty truths
which unbidden, arrive as rogue, unannounced, guests

The Cheaters

I spied a telepath or two on Pictionary
They are daring, disguised by the occasion's
razzmatazz televised excitement
Neither could draw and did not need to —
a squiggle, and angled dash, rendered
with a serious flourish, a fake forced look of consternation
'til the eager friend wastes no seconds to pronounce
the object's correct guess to the amazement of all.
A sweet hustle. You must be somewhat telegenic
and Californian, as there is not yet a way to test
and exclude your psychic cheating skills

Irish

for mind reader is léitheoir intinne (reader of the mind)

Failed Spy

I was not effective as a spy
no matter how diligently I tried
ever barraged by peregrinations of devious minds
whose lies were truths and truths were lies

all held tightly woven, dense, belief baskets
which carried water in searing desert heat
shifting patterned kufis doused with subtle perfumes
made me dizzy, eye slits-only reveals left me weighted in covert

I am not a man, which helped greatly to be faceless domestic help,
avoid hurt, unseen and unsuspected, a small shift in demeanor
or attitude left me undetected for minor gatherings of intelligence
to confirm, fact find, fill files, inform, invisibly present,
but I wanted to expand my scope, do so much wondrous more,
extend my reach and range, explore our hidden, ruling world

Untangle large intricacies of state crafts' tightrope moves:
tread the dizzying high above, check deep threats,
remove, destabilizing folks perched and primed to rule
before their fascist, autocratic reigns came true:
to hobble pustuled goblin feet of those who trod
upon the poor, our youth, any and all those othered.

But alas, my deep skill has no range. I can't see what's coming.
unless it's a lit train – I can feel some vibration through the Earth
through psychic rails, down dark, glistening track,
yet so can most folks, for a telepath to be a stunning,
cunning spy, there's little good with merely that

Rabbit

So many dark country nights from the airport
driving home alone on empty highway
huge trucks hurtling cityward in the far lane

In these wee hours deer might dare
Though I said no, no
ahead I saw a rabbit hopping across
moved right to the lane it had passed

rabbit bound back the way it had come
I guessed wrong or sent wrong
our collision made no sound

I did not look back or slow, seeing only
the growing glare of lights behind me
hurtful end of a business trip

Romeo and Juliet
for Obi

Night after night a new habit:
cat sitting at the front door,
prickled her 'til she saw
the source of cat's attention

An elongated, pale pink nosed face,
with whiskers sprouting askew, distorted
rat thing with naked, puke-beige, ridge-ringed tail,
looking squat, and pleading on the other side of the door,

right there where scent might slip out or in
under, through the door sweep,
and she shrieked and yelled,
breaking their love spell

How could her beauty be charmed by such a beast?
Black bead eyes, rolled up, pleaded
as her horror thundered down upon it,
driving it away from her unopened door

She later learned all the good opossums do
their steady serving quietude, saving lives, eating tics
became ashamed of what she had thought at it
and her cat mourned its love
lost to stupid human thoughts

Cat Dreams
for Obi and Niles

Her dynamic fur duo didn't care
much for each other, though for her
sake, they shared space, vied
for attention subtly, cooperated
in urging her to do things on their
peculiar schedule: out in and in out
annoyingly endearing pauses by doors

She tried to hear them or tell them,
but they knew only what they wanted
rarely broke ranks, ignored her 'til needed

One day she woke, startled, confused,
by dream like soft static, greased lenses
on a slow locomotive, moving through
a blurred, undefined terrain, muffled hum

her mouth felt full of feathers,
and she sputtered awake to four eyes
staring smugly: contact achieved
She never napped around them again,
made sure to shut her bedroom door

everything transmits
can you receive? are you tuned?
many frequencies

MIND
IDEA
NEAT
DATE

Debridement

Each week they told T it was necessary
to encourage the wound to heal
As they used a melon scoop tool
to remove flesh from her heel
And though the wound clinic
claimed its independence
the late arriving bill said it was
weekly outpatient surgery
from the hospital at its side

and the nurses disliked T's questions
and the harried, brown, pregnant doctor
demurred, deferred to her pale harridans
floating in and out of a consciousness
warped by worry and water weight

It was when the most venomous of them
declared she was going to Africa
to help and minister, that the true
horror in her mind wriggled into view

a spinning hatred of every insight
T revealed, T's unaged countenance,
T's persistence and T saw the hideous
history of those with sharp tools
cutting, cutting, cutting darker
flesh under the false flag of healing
and medicine, unfurl

WHO GOES THERE GOES THERE GOES THERE
WHO THERE GOES THERE WHO THERE WHO
GOES WHO THERE GOES WHO THERE GOES
THERE WHO GOES THERE WHO THERE
WHO THERE
GOES
THERE
WHO
THERE
WHO
THERE
WHO
THERE
WHO
GOES

Telepath's Guy

She was always confused, he said
mistaking words, he did not hear
what she heard when they socialized

The blandest statement might surprise her
some minor announcement could astound
or offhand quip, enrage her

Make her eyes narrow and brow crease
as she removed herself to the kitchen
muttering about how dare that idiot

Or how momentous or portentous
some occasion truly was or would be
when she wrinkled her nose

as if something smelled badly
or her cat-like upper lip lift
one corner faintly twitching

Or when her ears rocked back
and upward, that time he said
he'd had to work late

He loved her, he thought, quirks
and all, *ha ha*, even though she knew better
always, always, discerningly right

Priestess
for Mama

She mothered and ministered
from her white stone counter
and frond-filled bay window seat
where huge leaved greens within canopied
colored sunlight, screened gray concrete

Some stood, others sat and poured out
their inexplicable needs that she held aloft
and healed somehow as if darning
a worn garment's frayed fabric or crocheting
small galaxies from cotton thread
humming safety nets and cures
of sweet dissipation or reinforcing endurance
just the sound of her throat clucks
miasma dispelling clicks, incisive, cleansing chipses

as soft light came from her
hovering above my growing head
I would nestle by her side
and see emanations rise
and drape shopper-supplicants who worshiped
at her grocery store. Every word she said
long lingering and forgotten,
holds me through these trembling dissolutions,
binds me still to that incalculable creative force

She, who represented God on earth,
manifesting unconditional love
worked daily outside the home
made she who made me, sailed
two monster-laden seas alone
carried Blue Mountain insights,
dreams from Saint Ann's to Harlem

freighter ship passenger list, said "Nurse"
revealing her training in healing, mediating,
helping others to recover, move forward
get better, be whole

SEEK
EASE
ESSE
KEEP

How This Is

I.

This wordless knowing dwells without a sound
arrives unasked, a sudden errant breeze.
A solar flare disturbs your atmosphere and leaves
you awed by light displays above mind's soggy ground
that signal forces yet unknown to which you're bound
which tug and roil as tides furrow earth's seas.
So others' thoughts crack and crowd as spring ice heaves.
They press the mind's slim channels and surround
your own internal flow, your own untrammeled way
though guessing's less and insight grows with each
connection made, yet still not all is clearly displayed.
Clear understanding is what you hope to reach
though rarely do their thoughts match what they say
there's space between what's known and what they preach.

II.

The space between what's known and what they preach
grows wider with each struggle to achieve
what must be done for balance, to relieve
the pressures, stress that stunts our growth, betrays our reach
toward brighter probabilities, those great ideals we teach
our young, to shape them to evolve, make them believe
the greater possibilities they might someday achieve
that each and every grain of sand is needed for a beach
to honor precepts, those ideals that keep high hopes alive.
It aches to know that liars wish to truly mean what they say,
weigh stark options to decide if their better angels thrive.
Which dirtied, muddied truth will hold sway
to build consensus, or decide which concern will be denied
and high ideals, made low, are packed away.

III.

And high ideals made low, and packed away
like old luggage, grandma's red trunk, disguised, re-dressed
as furnishing, covered by cloth or board – who'd guess
what was stored in plain sight beneath a tray?
What mean debris sat central, awaiting the light of day?
It might appear like this, if thoughts were so expressed
but seldom are they so clear, they're generally a mess.
Cluttered expanses, barely rooms, dance with fog and gray
barely defined, most are half-formed and unclear
wordless, jangled, bits and pieces, they arrive.
Few hold concepts, just what they hold dear
or, in conversing, don't want said, but want to hide
and even that degrades with false bravado or pulsing fear
so I can't decipher much from this shifting, sticky outside.

IV.

I can't decipher deeply from this shifting, sticky outside
enough arrives, yet how, I can't detect.
The past said I can not receive as well as I can project
when in my youth long distance was tried
but close range insights can't be denied.
We know more about ourselves, we water electric
and less about how our collective connects
as ritual remembrances dream time provides
among those indigenous protectors of sacred knowings.
Perhaps they better understand this process
once helpful to coordinate our comings and goings
before technology provided another access
for those who lost their skills by industries' growing,
consuming fertile unspoiled land, lost for progress.

V.

Consuming fertile unspoiled land, lost for progress
did industry slaughter our connection
the death of folkways, rural rejection
in gaining more products have we lost this process?
This basic, now mystic human congress
by which we join beyond kinship and affection
each to the other with prelinguistic ease, without rejection.
I have just the remnants of that to use, to guess.
It wavers, quavers, flickers as senses go
less steady, not always ready, lightning strike
blue blaze crackling through my skull, and sometimes slow.
Other senses, data, may clue this unheard insight.
Yet others, unveiled, wonder at the depth of known
untold, unseen, unasked, revealed, their hidden light.

VI.

Untold, unseen, unasked, revealed, their hidden light
aides, agencies, close enough to smell or see
passersby, door ringers, whoever they may be
any who fall within my pulsing sphere, my sight

Triggered to delve when their hate or slights
disguised as query, rank discourse assaults me
prevaricating jive, microagressive sprees
billow from so many like a nanoparticle blight

My family knew when I faced life-threatening fear
when college men threatened death, when I nearly slid off a hill
though I never told, they felt shed skin, felt me forbear
all those Ivy-leagued ways I was nearly killed
baby sister complained this link brought pain to them there,
their weight-bearing lessened the load and helps me still

VII.

Their weight-bearing lessened the load and helps me still
reverberating ancestral protection across the years
survivors of multi-centuried genocides, forged from tears
invisible armors of love and prescient mythic wills.

They worked their way from sea to sea and filled
their children's souls with strength and transcendent care
nourished by a shorn, remembered radiance and shared
an unsurrendered power, a vestigial, invisible skill

that deep within me quietly resides
and signals forces yet unknown to which I'm bound.
I pay homage, pray, grateful this golden core abides
encircles me in a radiant, protective surround
rests, awaits threat or peril to again arise:
this wordless knowing dwells without a sound.

Transit Called Dreaminess

A Mercury Sextile Neptune

In your contacts with people
you have a much clearer sense
of what is going on in others' minds.

If you can keep your perception
straight in your head,
you will be astonished
by the insights about people
that this influence can bring.

You should not try
to use your rational mind
very much. Rely
more on your inner
senses and feelings.

Your senses become acute
you pick up much
extra information through intuition

The Singer

Don't close your eyes, they say
the singer must connect with the audience

They do not know the pain she tries to avoid
that closing her eyes is just a way
to manage the toothed tsunami of screaming
light shards hurtling from the many eyes trained
upon her as she stands trembling slightly on stage

Some indifferent, some annoyed, some amused,
some angry, some ravenous with expectation
and some, with one look, already disappointed
How could she sing with her eyes open?
so much comes in from her unnamed sense

> *She can hear their burbling guts,*
> *the food they ate, their discomforts*
> *and satiations, bladder shifts, and wrigglings*
> *below and above their belts, radiations*
> *of desires wafting, all expressed as smellsoundtastethought*

She has learned to transmit,
but not how to filter what shoots toward her
at her, so she sings with her eyes
closed until the moment her song
and their body sounds braid frequencies
into something endurable, a soft ladder
she might clamber up and better yet
an old wooden escalator on which they all stand
on which they can all ascend

So her shut-eyed beginnings remain unchanged
until she gains more skill, more power
to reach and gather the audience of wild, disparate minds
flailing in their separateness, yearning for wholeness
then she can look, let them in, and lead them out

Portal

I can send you my too-big shirt,
my uneaten romaine lettuce and unplanted seeds,
You can help me weed my yard
wheel me to consuming bush so i can reach
a respite from too early cold for me
and from searing Saharan heat for you
see the wet Chemung river rise
as I watch sand dune shifts,
mediate threats that encroach
a vacation for us, both
from neighbors who wage war on us
cattle thieves, where your settlement
is under siege, and my bullet-ridden house bleeds
care packages raided by porch thieves
chant with me, oh distant friend
this right adjusting frequency
open our inner temples
we will heal
wound by wound
this transition

Ignite

Hold open a place before exhale,
a readied pause between cricket chirps sounds sequence
peppering lamp lit night with signal timpanies
smell these tiny songs sparking micro ignitions
behind eyelids when your ears' hunger goes
unfed, what that signifies is not language
loves signal flares of fireflies, rustle of leaf stir
light-walkers cross dimensions to brush your consciousness
awake to lightning strikes behind eyelids
listen with another organ unnamed, untamed, waiting
in your unused chunk of brain and sleeping DNA

Encompass

Sunshine is frequently crooked
and windows have certainties. Fireflies
make cold light on warm evenings.
I let go of designations that end futures.
The next epoch will be kinder. I am a spaceship
dreaming of landing on Mars, conveying the hopeful.
I was a woman without heels who could only roll swiftly
downhill. Inclines require assistance, power or knowledge.
Curb cuts are too steep. Strength is best bent. Sentience is not a gift
when you are stuffed in a box, braying and crying for
a red release or green expanse. I track dust and mud prints
on shiny floors and yearn for a wise trajectory. Travesties
are too soon forgotten. Clouds obscure as does fog
but weather is local until it's not. Finitude can comfort
or constrain. This too shall pass. Scarcity is a falsehood of
        imprisonments.
Skidmarks are signs of consumption. Shred, repurposed, dispossessed,
this is how I'm made useful.

T- Stroll

Thoughts fly, flail, flagellate, fill you unbidden
Ever present energies engaging your innards
Lingering as you move past others, through crowds, down streets
Enticing glimpses into many minds, all sentience radiating
Pathways to enter, mystic meridians to follow, qi linked
Access to multiplicities of nows, a flooding roar of perceptions
Traveling along gossamer energy lines, floating errant web strings
Hindering your walkabout, healing your singularity,
                    your singularity

Acknowledgments

"My Mother, She Ate Me" was previously published in *FIYAH* in January 2023 and won the 2024 IGNYTE Award for Best Poem.

"Encompass" was previously published in *About Place Journal,* Fall 2022.

"Guessing Weight" was previously published in *Tiny Moments Volume III,* Bronze Bird Books, David Pring-Mill, editor, May 2024.

"First Contact" and "Babel" were published in *Martian Wave*, March 2025.

My unswerving gratitude to:

Dr. Nistico and the hyperbaric team, Jessica and Ashley, who worked
to save my life and held space for my true self to heal
my beloved cousin, Dana Holland, for being an earth angel
Andrea Bempong for rescuing me from the nursing home
the departed Anton Besterbreurtje for enabling me to return to my home
Judy Serkin for pinch hitting
all the wonderful folks who funded my wheelchair
my Beloved Departed who enable me to survive to this moment, hurtling me forward.

Telepath Notes

In the late 1960s, I participated in long distance ESP experiments conducted by the American Society for Psychical Research, whose journals I read as a teenager: *Proceedings of the American Society for Psychical Research* and *Journal of the American Society for Psychical Research*. They were headquartered in Manhattan; I lived with my family in Queens.

WBSU, The Black Student Union at Williams College, was located in the basement of Mears House in the 1970s.

Project Stargate was a secret US government program/army unit that investigated the potential military and domestic intelligence applications of psychic phenomena such as remote viewing and extrasensory perception (ESP). The program was active from the 1970s to 1995.

Queens is a borough of New York City, which in my youth was considered "country" for its many un- or poorly-paved streets, large undeveloped green spaces and single family homes. It was a place a number of black celebrities made home, including John Coltrane and Count Basie, also the area in which America's first black poet, Jupiter Hammon, was born.

Big Flats (f. 1822) is a town in Chemung County, NY, west of the city of Elmira. The Chemung River flows through the southern part of town. It is a river valley whose geography includes a broad expanse of relatively flat land wreathed by hills, historically known for its tobacco. Fossil seashells indicate the land was an ancient sea bottom. The Harris Hill Soaring Museum is there. The hills around create thermals used by the gliders.

Microacrostics were taught to me in the mid-1970's by the poet Thomas Elias Weatherly, whose book, *MauMau American Cantos* had been taught by Professor/Poet Larry Neal when I attended Williams College.

Films

Nightmare Alley was a film I watched long ago with my mother, who loved films of a bygone era, and saw again as an adult It had resonance for me back in the day for "I married Joan" ('What a girl, what a pearl what a wife') Joan Blondell of TV was in the film, as was the dashing Tyrone Power. I realize that I didn't remember how it ended, memory cutting the film off after the penultimate act of betrayal. I watched the Guillermo del Toro remake without memory of the childhood film, more slick and glamorous, edgy and stylized and still compelling in its karmic undertones, its strange familiarity not a déjà vu, but remembering.

Scanners (1981) is a Canadian sci-fi film written and directed by David Cronenberg. Scanners were psychics with telepathic and telekinetic abilities. An arms firm named ConSec hunts scanners. A renegade scanner wages war against ConSec while another scanner is sent by the firm to stop him.

SENSE8 (2015-2018) is a film/video television series created by Lana and Lilly Wachowski and J. Michael Straczynski* (adore him) for Netflix about a pod of telepaths around the world who assist each other through their ability to share/inhabit/inform each other with their skills and insights. They are, of course, propelled by a killing opposition that searches for them and arms/weaponizes various institutional systems in an attempt to destroy them. But there is strength in the collective and its allies.

THE FURY (1978) is a movie written by John Farris, directed by Brian De Palma, in which Kirk Douglas plays a former CIA agent who employs Amy Irving to assist him in rescuing his telekinetic son played by Andrew Stevens from a secret US agency led by John Cassavetes which steals children with parapsychological abilities and weaponizes them. I recall being deeply moved by this — remembering the father's efforts to save his son and Amy Irving's portrayal as a heroic rescuer.

*J. Michael Straczynski was the creator of the grand space opera television series *Babylon 5* which ran for 5 seasons from 1994 to 1998. This sweeping series was unerringly compelling and the role of the telepaths and the Psi-Corps were among its many wondrous story arcs.

Childhood Books

The People by Zenna Henderson

The Whole Man (1964) is a sci-fi novel by John Brunner and was nominated for a Hugo Award for Best Novel in 1965. It was published under the title *Telepathist* in the UK.

Collective Nouns

a brainstorm of telepaths

an embrace of telepaths

an influence of telepaths

an insight of telepaths

a relay of telepaths

a sea of telepaths

a silence of telepaths

a surround of telepaths

a sweep of telepaths

a theory of telepaths

a thought swarm of telepaths

a warp of telepaths

a wave of telepaths

a weave of telepaths

a weft of telepaths

About the Author

A third generation African-Caribbean New Yorker, firstborn, wisdom seeker, creator, and paraplegic, Akua Lezli Hope has won a Creative Writing Fellowship from The National Endowment for The Arts, two Artists Fellowships from the New York Foundation for the Arts, a Ragdale U.S.-Africa Fellowship, and three artist grants from the New York State Council on the Arts.

In 2022 she was named a Grand Master of Fantastic Poetry by the Science Fiction and Fantasy Poetry Association (SFPA). She has won scholarships for the Hurston Wright writers' program and the Provincetown Fine Arts Work Center. She is a Cave Canem fellow.

Her art and poetry card project, Words on Wheels, which delivered them to the homebound elderly, won an Artists Grant. She received an Artists Crossroads Grant from The Arts Council of the Southern Finger Lakes for her project "Words in Motion," which placed poetry on the buses of New York's Chemung and Steuben counties.

Her first collection, **EMBOUCHURE, Poems on Jazz and Other Musics,** won the Writer's Digest book award for poetry. Her collection, **Them Gone,** a finalist in the Word Works Washington Prize competition, was published in 2018 by The Word Works. Her speculative poetry chapbook, **Otherwheres**, won the 2021 Elgin award.

She has received multiple Best of the Net, Rhysling, and Dwarf Star nominations Her poems, Montserrat and Awaiting Your Return (for Jamal Kashoggi) were nominated for a 2019 Pushcart Prize. Her poem "Metis Emits" won a Science Fiction and Fantasy Poetry Association's short poem award. She has twice won Rattle's Poet's Respond. Her poem, "Giant Robot and his Person" won the 27th Annual Critters Readers' Poll Best Poem. Her poem, "My mother, she ate me" won the 2024 IGNYTE Award for Best Poem. Her poem, Igbo Landing II, won a Rhysling Long Poem Award.

She created and has hosted the renowned Speculative Sundays Poetry Reading Series from 2020 to date.

She created the historic, groundbreaking, first anthology of BIPOC speculative poetry, **NOMBONO**, published by Sundress Publications, and edited the largest ever issue of Eye to the Telescope, on The Sea.

She has been in print since 1974 with over 500 poems published in numerous literary magazines and national anthologies including: **Bestiary of Blood, Black Joy Unbound, Black Fire this Time (2022), Wreaths for a Wayfarer: An Anthology in Honour of Pius Adesanmi, Eccentric Orbits Volume 2, Revise the Psalm: Work Celebrating the Writing of Gwendolyn Brooks, The Crafty Poet II: A Portable Workshop, Too Much Boogie, Erotic Remixes of the Dirty Blues, The 100 Best African American Poems, The Year's Best Writing**, Writer's Digest Guides; **THE BLUELIGHT CORNER**, black women writing on passion, sex, and romantic love; **Will Work For Peace**: New Political Poems; **SISTERFIRE**, an anthology of Black Womanist Fiction and Poetry, ed. by Charlotte Watson-Sherman; **WHAT IS FOUND THERE, NOTEBOOKS ON POETRY AND POLITICS** by Adrienne Rich, W.W. Norton; **WRITING FROM THE NEW COAST: TECHNIQUE**, Buffalo University; **EROTIQUE NOIRE**, (the first!) AN ANTHOLOGY OF BLACK EROTICA, Doubleday/Anchor; **POETS MARKET,** ed. by Judson Jerome, Writers Digest Books; **CONFIRMATION**, an anthology of Afrikan American Women Writers; **EXTENDED OUTLOOKS**, the Iowa Review Collection of Contemporary Women Writers; **Nature Triumphs** Anthology, **Space Funk** anthology, **50 over 50**, About Place Journal, African American Review, Blue Cage (England),Breath and Shadow, Catalyst, Catalyst, CHAIN, Contact II, Dreams and Nightmares, Earth's Daughters 52, Eye to the Telescope, Eyeball, Faerie Magazine, Fantasy and Science Fiction Magazine, Gramarye, Hambone II, Iron Horse Review, Killens Review, Lockjaw Magazine,

MASKS, Minerva Rising, New Verse News, Obsidian II, Pensive Journal, Penumbra, Poets Reading the News, Raising Mothers Magazine, Rattle, Scifaikuest, Silver Blade, SpecPoVerse, Sublimation, synkroniciti, SoFi (Sociological Fiction), Star*line, Stone Canoe, Strange Horizons, The Cossack Review, The Crafty Poet II, Three Coyotes, Tiny Text, among many others.

She was a finalist in the Open Voice competition, in the Barnard New Women Poets Series with her manuscript Fuel for Beginners, and in the MacDonald's Black literary competition. Her collection, The Prize is the Journey, was a finalist in the Walt Whitman contest.

UNPACKING, her collaboration with dancer choreographer, Lois Welk, was presented in 2003 at 171 Cedar Arts Center. She was a poet-in-residence at the Chautauqua Institute where she read her poetry, lectured on jazz poetry, and conducted a workshop entitled "Writing Poetry as Mythmaking."

Akua also writes speculative short fiction which has been included in: **Afrofuturism Anthology** (Flametree), **Africa Risen** (Tor), **For Those Who Deserve to Exist** (Inked in Gray Press, 2022), **Open Minds,** (Shreyer) and **DARK MATTER**, (the first!) anthology of African American Science Fiction, (Time Warner Books).

She holds a B.A. in psychology from Williams College, a M.B.A. in marketing from Columbia University Graduate School of Business, and a M.S.J. in broadcast journalism from Columbia University Graduate School of Journalism.

Her collection of senryu, **Our 50th** (ArtFarm Press), commemorates her experience as being among the first class including women at Williams College.

She was a founding section leader in the Poetry Forum on Compuserve. She served as a founding section leader of the African American Resource Forum and in the Books and Writers section of the African American Culture Forum (American Visions) on Compuserve. She also served as a trainer, area coordinator, and group founder and leader for Amnesty International, U.S.A., in the Southern Tier of New York. She co-authored a biweekly column on social, political, and cultural issues for the Star Gazette.

She is a founding member of the Black Writers Union and the New Renaissance Writers Guild whose alumni include Arthur Flowers, Walter Dean Myers and Terri McMillan.

She led the Voices of Fire Reading Choir from 1987 to 1999, performing her work and that of other African American poets. Akua has given hundreds of readings to audiences in colleges, prisons, parks, museums, libraries and bars.

Akua founded a paratransit nonprofit, awaiting a vehicle, to provide transportation for the wheelchair bound in her tiny town.

Akua also creates sculpture, objects, and jewelry in glass, fiber, metal, concrete and handmade paper; has published over 130 crochet patterns; plays the soprano saxophone; sings animé tunes in Japanese; and makes good manifest.

Praise for *TELEPATH*

In TELEPATH, Akua Lezli Hope maps the electric meridians of the unspoken, tracing a "wordless knowing" that hums within the blood long before a phone rings or a mouth opens. There is a deep, startling intelligence in these poems, a clarity that looks straight into the eyes of the world and wins. With a quiet, vulnerable beauty, Hope's language acts as a solar flare in the mind's atmosphere, illuminating the ancestral oneness we nearly forgot. A stunning, visionary work.

Sheree Renée Thomas, multi-award winning author of *The Tongue I Dream In,* editor of The Magazine of Fantasy and Science Fiction

With *TELEPATH* we see a grandmaster of speculative poetry firmly in her element, providing an excellent introduction to her technique and literary priorities that are at once compelling, personal and deeply imaginative. Each line and turn of phrase is fine-tuned to launch you across an epic trajectory of the outermost boundaries of language and perception, managing to look internally and externally at once. From pieces like "First Contact" and "My mother she ate me" to her closing poem "T-Stroll" Akua Lezli Hope adds a wonderful set of poems to the world sure to inspire and delight the curious reader.

Bryan Thao Worra, Science Fiction and Fantasy Poetry Association President (2016-2022)

In award-winning poet Akua Lezli Hope's speculative collection, *TELEPATH*, we are transported inside what it is to experience others' emotions, thoughts, as well as communication between telepaths. Akua's poems give a kaleidoscope of views on having an ability that can be used to gain and lose relationships, identity, money or to be a telepath enslaved who may not know the language being spoken, but has a deep knowing of the slaver's intention. We can imagine how it feels to know the difference between what is said and the truth inside a person. A variety of poetry forms gracefully move words on the page, carrying us through the challenges of a gift that can bring maddening loneliness or wonderful companionship. I was fascinated by the idea of us all being telepaths, once upon a time.

Linda D. Addison, award-winning
author, HWA Lifetime Achievement
Award recipient and SFPA Grand
Master

Hope transmits a poetic philosophical explosion for the sixth sense. *TELEPATH* takes us on a trip from birth to the outer reaches of the cosmos to New York, and through dimensions only visible to those who look with the third eye. Hope's words are music transferred from mind to mind, so open up and receive.

Jean-Paul L. Garnier, owner of Space Cowboy
Books, Editor-in-Chief of Electronic Brain
Magazine